BUTTERFLIES

collected in

the

Shire Valley, East Africa

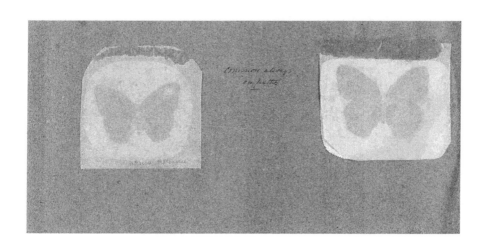

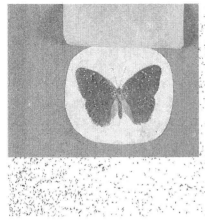

Common always
on paths.

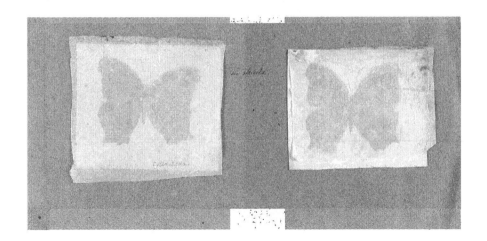

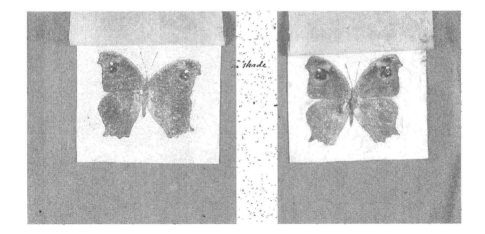

shade

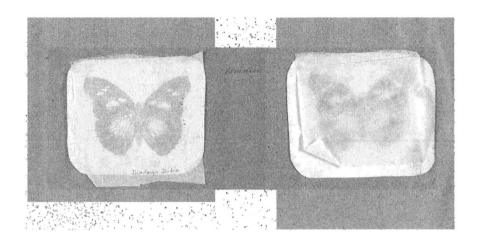

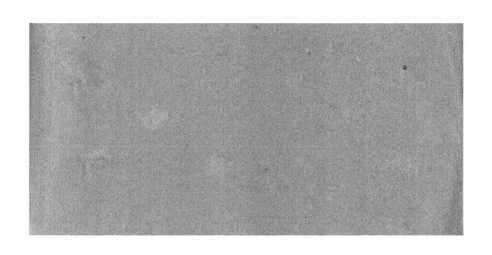

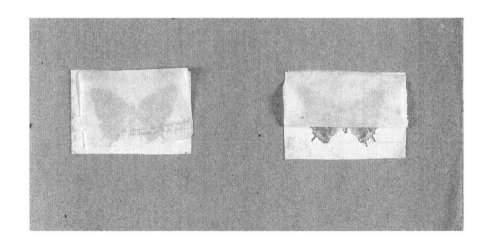

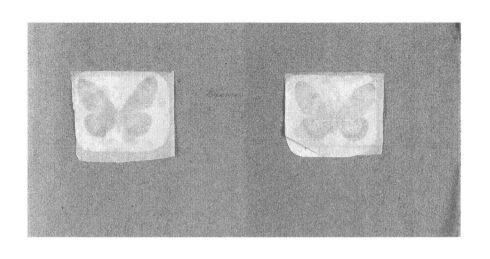

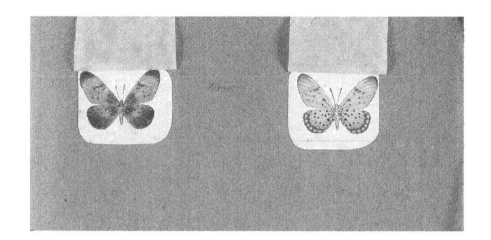

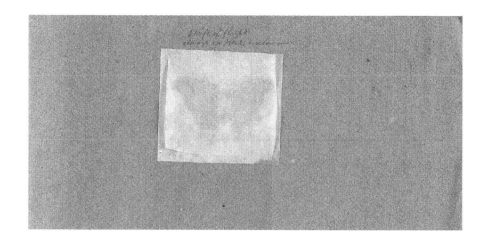

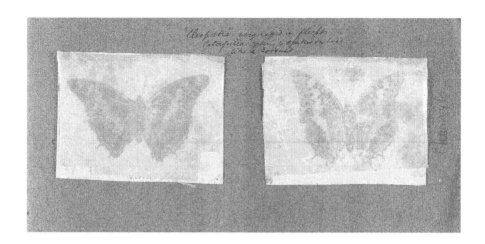

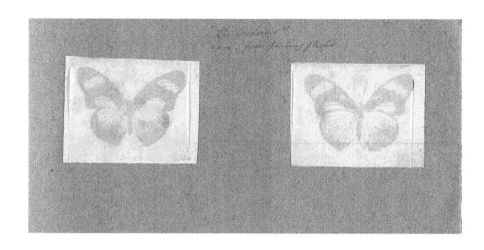

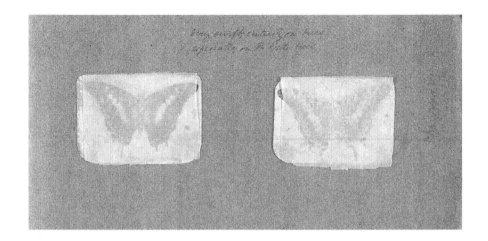

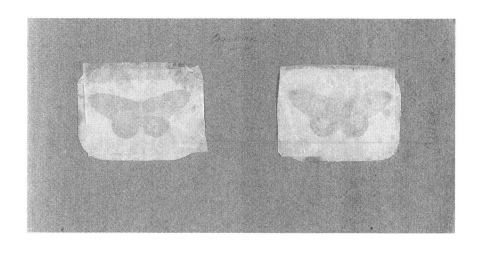

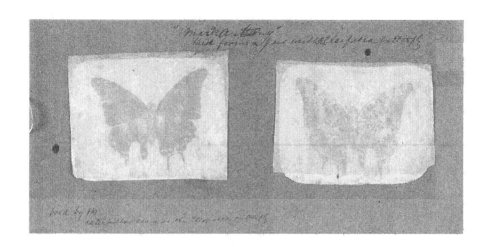

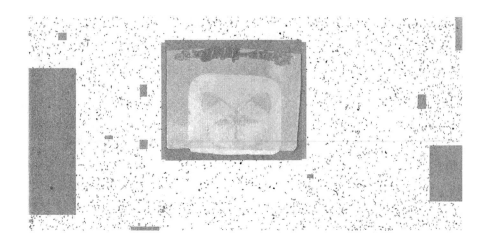

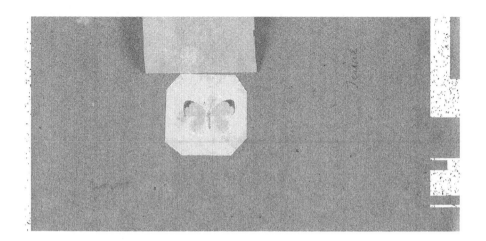

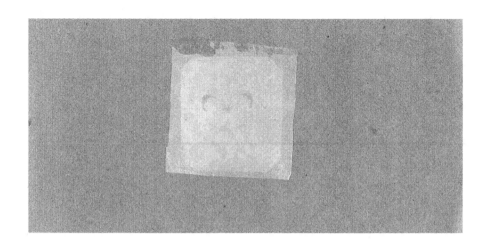

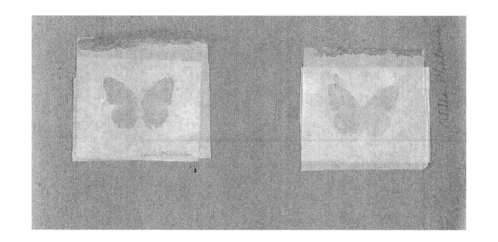

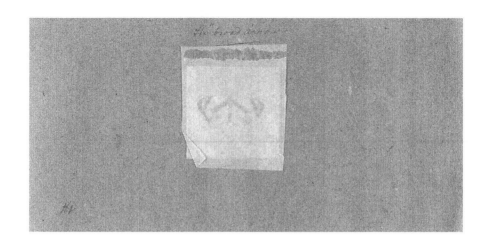

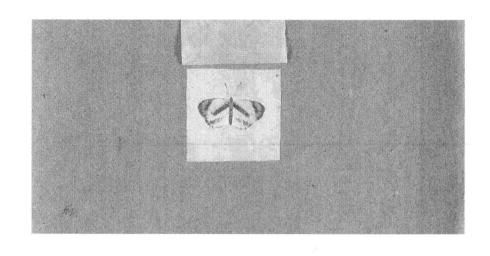

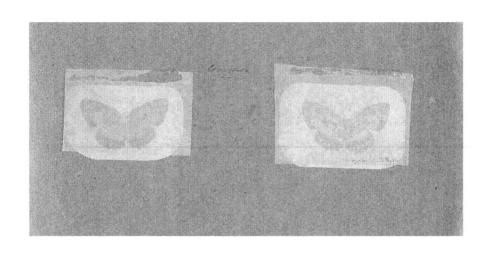

The colours in the tips it should be mauve but as this too't first as only one of the colours that compose it is reproduced. I could not match it exactly.

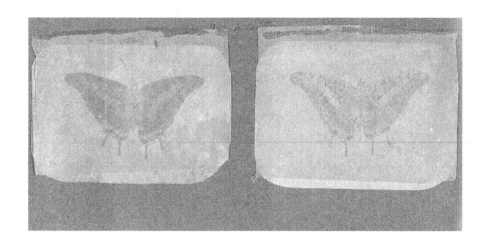

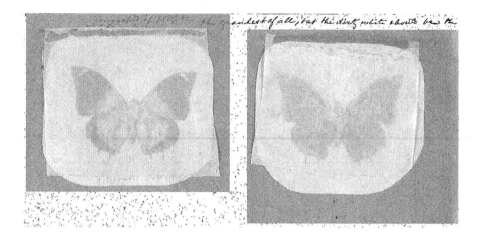

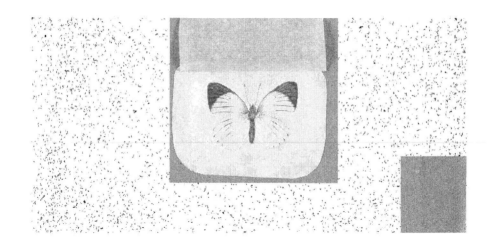

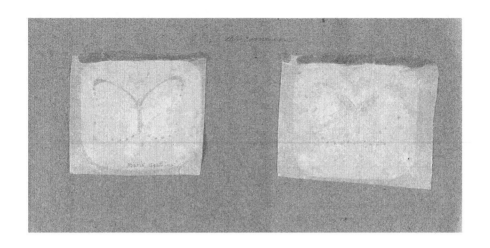

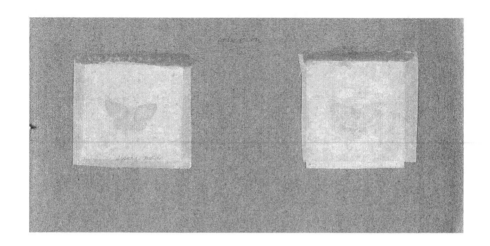

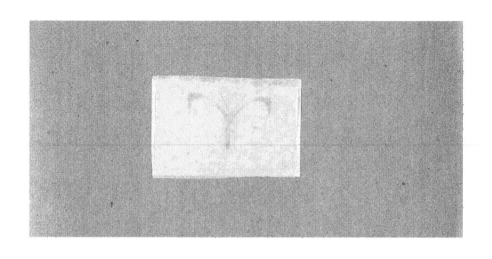

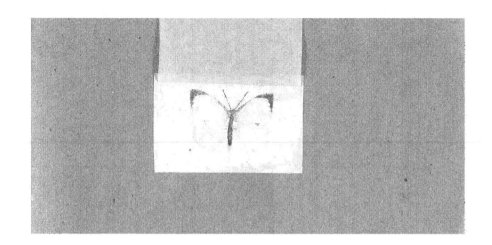

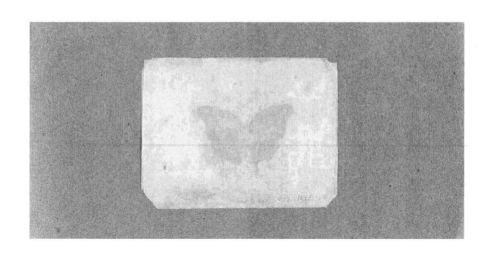

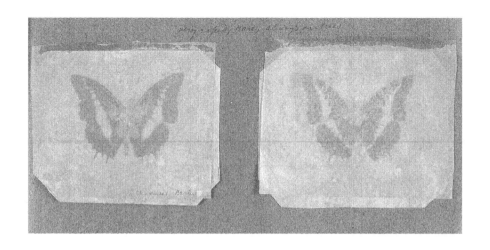

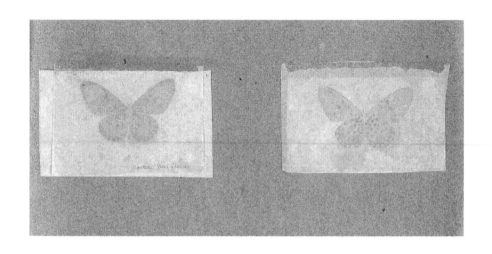

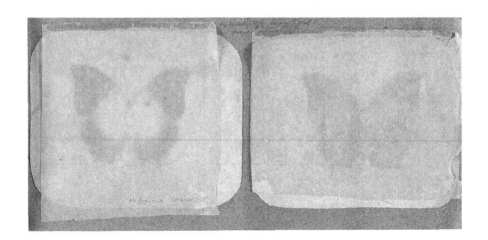

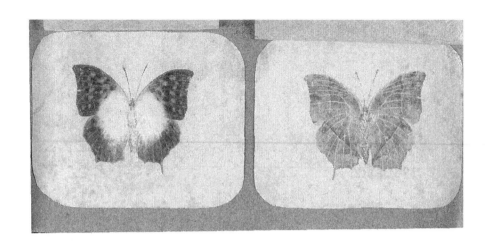

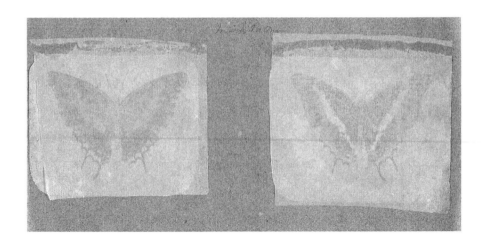

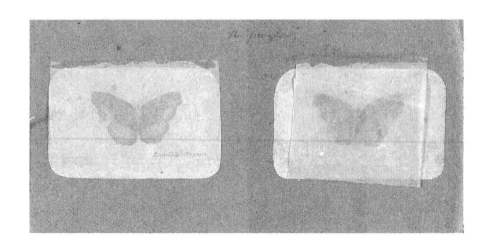

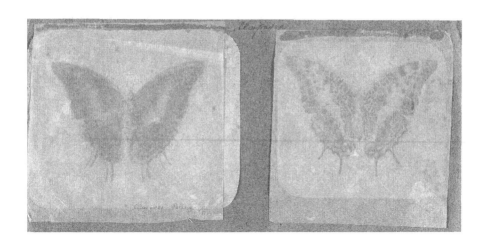

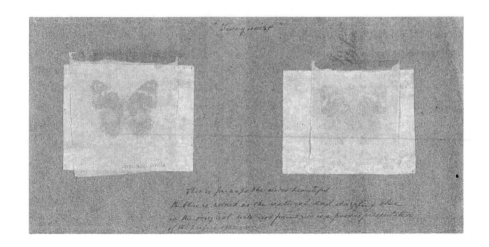

"Conquerer"

There is perhaps the most beautiful
of the blue related as the natural deep dazzling blue
in the original both near painted, it is possibly a representation
of the perfect specimen

Turquoise

This is perhaps the most beautiful
of blue as milled as the material, and dazzling blue
in the very life, till not painted in a few negligibled
of the purple ground plan.